DATE DUE

Galileo

Paul Mason

Heinemann Library
Chicago, Illinois

© 2001 Reed Educational & Professional Publishing
Published by Heinemann Library,
an imprint of Reed Educational & Professional Publishing,
Chicago, IL
Customer Service 888-454-2279
Visit our website at www.heinemannlibrary.com

Designed by Elaine Hewson
Illustrated by Michael Posen
Originated by Ambassador Litho
Printed in Hong Kong/China

05 04 03 02 01
10 9 8 7 6 5 4 3 2 1

Library of Congress Cataloging-in-Publication Data
Mason, Paul, 1967-
    Galileo / Paul Mason.
        p. cm. -- (Groundbreakers)
    Includes bibliographical references and index.
    ISBN 1-58810-052-9 (lib. bdg.)   ISBN 1-58810-991-7 (pbk. bdg.)
    1. Galilei, Galileo, 1564-1642--Juvenile literature. 2.
Astronomers--Italy--Biography--Juvenile literature. 3.
Physicists--Italy--Biography--Juvenile literature. [1. Galileo, 1564-1642. 2. Scientists.] I.
Title. II. Series.

    QB36.G2 .M42 2001
    520'.92---dc21
    [B]
                                                                    00-059682

Acknowledgments
The author and publishers are grateful to the following for permission to reproduce copyright material: AKG London, p. 10; AKG London/S. Dominie, pp. 21, 22, 24; AKG London/Erich Lessing, pp. 30, 36, 37, 40, 41; Bridgeman Art Library, p. 43; Corbis/Yann-Arthus Bertrand, p.14; Mary Evans Picture Library, pp. 6, 8, 16, 17, 20, 23, 27, 34, 35, 38; MPM Images, pp. 13, 19; Science and Society Picture Library/ Science Museum, pp. 5, 18, 26, 28, 29; Science Photo Library, pp. 4, 12, 25, 32, 39, 42.
Cover photograph reproduced with the permission of AKG London.

Some words are shown in bold, **like this.** You can find out what they mean by looking in the glossary.

Contents

Who Was Galileo?

Science as we know it barely existed when Galileo Galilei was born in 1564. At that time, universities were filled with learned people called **philosophers,** who followed the teachings of ancient Greeks such as Plato and Aristotle. Philosophers spent their time discussing ancient theories about how things might work, rather than performing experiments to prove how things truly worked.

Testing theories

Galileo rejected the traditional approach. He believed that before an idea could be accepted as true, it had to be tested and proven. This was one of his greatest contributions to modern science. Galileo's search for the truth involved him in some spectacular experiments. It is said that he once dropped balls of different sizes and weights from the top of a tower to demonstrate that the speed at which objects fall does not depend on their weight.

The ideas of this ancient Greek philosopher, Aristotle, dominated the universities of the seventeenth century. Galileo was one of the first scientists to move from just discussing theories, as Aristotle did, to carrying out experiments to test whether those theories are correct.

Famous in his lifetime

Galileo was as famous in his own time as he is today. He was a highly entertaining speaker, making his audience laugh at the same time as he made his opponents look foolish. He published many popular scientific books and performed public experiments, and his fame grew throughout his life. Galileo was also a great inventor. His inventions included powerful telescopes and early versions of the pocket calculator and **pendulum** clock.

Telescopes led Galileo to some of his greatest scientific discoveries. He made his own, which were more powerful than any others available at the time.

Galileo was also known for his attempts to show that the earth moved around the sun. Today this sounds obvious, but in the seventeenth century, this theory challenged what nearly everyone believed. By making the claim, Galileo angered many people. He faced the threat of imprisonment and torture; he made a bitter enemy of the pope, the head of the Catholic Church; and he even risked being sentenced to death.

Galileo's Early Years

This was Galileo's birthplace in Pisa, where he and his family lived until he was eight years old.

WHAT'S IN A NAME?

Like many Italian parents at the time, Galileo's decided to give him a name that was similar to the family name. Galileo's name was important in another way: it remembered Galileo Bonaiuti, a famous doctor after whom the whole family had been renamed during the fourteenth century. Galileo's fame grew throughout his lifetime, and today he is known simply by his first name.

Galileo was born in Pisa, Tuscany, on February 15, 1564. He was the first son of Vincenzio and Giulia Galilei. The family was originally from Florence, the capital city of the Tuscany region, but Galileo's father worked in Pisa as a musician. He also did experiments on **harmony.**

Although the Galilei had once been one of the most powerful families in Florence, by the time Galileo was born, his parents were short of money. Members of a well-known family such as the Galilei were expected to dress well, eat well, and maintain a high standard of living, and keeping up this lifestyle was expensive. Throughout Galileo's childhood, his family was constantly struggling for money.

In 1572, when Galileo was eight years old, his parents returned to their home city of Florence. Galileo stayed on with relatives in Pisa for two years. There is no record of why Galileo's parents left him in Pisa, but at the time it was not unusual for children to live with relatives for long periods. Galileo was finally reunited with his mother and father in Florence at the age of ten.

A Change of Direction

In the fall of 1581, at the age of seventeen, Galileo left home to go to the University of Pisa. Here, he followed the wishes of his father and studied medicine for two years. While he was studying at Pisa, Galileo noticed a chandelier swinging like a **pendulum.** He used his pulse to time the swings. But it was not until much later that he realized the full potential of the pendulum's time-keeping properties.

This was the Galilei family home in Florence. Galileo lived here from age ten to age seventeen, and again when he returned from the university.

In 1583, Galileo first came across the **geometry** studies of the Greek mathematician Euclid. Galileo fell in love with mathematics and abandoned his medical studies, much to his father's displeasure. Eventually, in 1585, Galileo returned home to his father's house with two years of medical studies and two years of mathematical studies behind him. But he had no degree, and he did not have any real job prospects, either.

Earning a living

Despite his lack of formal qualifications, Galileo taught mathematics to private students. He was unable to get a university teaching job. He wrote papers on geometry and gave public lectures. Galileo also took part in public discussions with other mathematicians and **philosophers,** and began to gain a reputation as a tough opponent in an argument.

Education

When he arrived in Florence, Galileo began to attend a local school, where he improved his reading and writing as well as studying other subjects such as **philosophy** and history. When he was thirteen, Galileo's father arranged for him to go to a **monastery** run by a strict religious order. Here his higher education began, and Galileo had to study the subjects that were expected of a gentleman, including Greek, Latin, and **logic.** These would also be useful in the career Vincenzio had picked out for his son: medicine.

While at the monastery, Galileo decided that he wanted to join the order of monks, but his father would not allow it. Money was almost certainly the reason. For Galileo to join the monastery, Vincenzio would have had to make a large initial payment, and then continue to pay for Galileo's upkeep for the rest of his life. Galileo's father had two daughters and two sons to provide for. The Galilei family needed their oldest son to become a money-earning doctor, not a further drain on their funds.

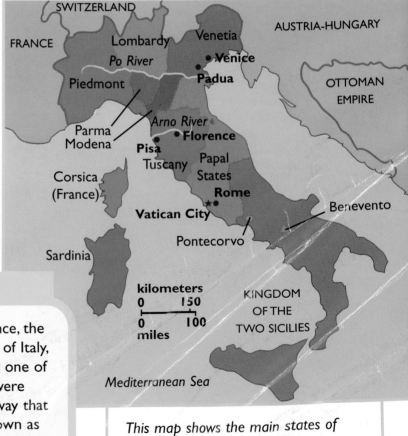

THE ITALIAN STATES

Galileo's family came from Florence, the capital of Tuscany. Today, it is part of Italy, but in Galileo's time, Tuscany was one of several independent states that were loosely called Italy (in the same way that Italy today is part of a region known as Europe).

This map shows the main states of Italy, which became one country in 1860–61.

LA BILANCETTA

While he lived at his father's house, Galileo invented a delicate method of weighing tiny objects accurately. It was a **hydrostatic balance**—a device that used water as a **counterweight**—called *La Bilancetta,* meaning "the little balance." A metal ball at one end sank into a cup of water, making the level of water rise or fall, depending on the weight of the object on the other side of the balance.

The manufacture and sale of the hydrostatic balances provided some extra money for the family, in addition to Vincenzio's and Galileo's teaching incomes.

From 1588 to 1589, Galileo worked part-time as his father's assistant. Vincenzio was investigating how **harmony** works. He had filled a whole room with weighted strings of various lengths, diameters, and **tensions,** to see if there was a relationship

between each of these things and the noise the strings made when plucked. This experience must have affected Galileo, who continued for the rest of his life to test his ideas through practical demonstrations.

Galileo performed many experiments himself around this time with balls, levers, pendulums, and other objects. He was interested in how they floated, fell, or swung. Galileo measured and timed the motions of these objects. Then he tried to work out mathematical explanations for how they moved, a method that modern scientists still use today.

In Galileo's words:

"The Universe cannot be read until we have learned the language in which it is written. It is written in mathematical language, and the letters are triangles, circles, and other geometrical figures."

(Galileo, in *The Assayer*)

Galileo's Fame Grows

This is the opening illustration of Dante's Inferno. Galileo gave talks on the mathematics of this book's version of hell, winning himself much admiration in Florence.

Tired of scratching out a living by teaching private students, and driven perhaps by the desire to make a greater name for himself, Galileo applied for a teaching post at the University of Bologna in 1588. He did not get the job, but his public lectures were starting to win him fame in Florence. Later on that year, Galileo was invited to deliver a lecture to the Florentine Academy, a group of wealthy citizens who were interested in literature. Galileo was asked to speak about the mathematics of *The Inferno*. This is part of an epic poem, *The Divine Comedy*, written in the fourteenth century by the famous Italian writer, Dante. It describes how hell is arranged in circles, each with its own dreadful characteristics. The lecture was a success, and Galileo was asked back to talk again.

Galileo's fame as a public speaker began to spread, and he was becoming well known as a brilliant mathematician, too. He had written several articles describing his ideas on centers of **gravity** that fell into the hands of a nobleman named Guidobaldo del Monte.

Del Monte was a mathematician who had written several books on **mechanics,** and he was instantly impressed with Galileo's ideas. With del Monte's help, in 1589 Galileo managed to get a job teaching mathematics at the University of Pisa. He packed up his possessions and began the short journey west, toward the city at the mouth of the Arno River.

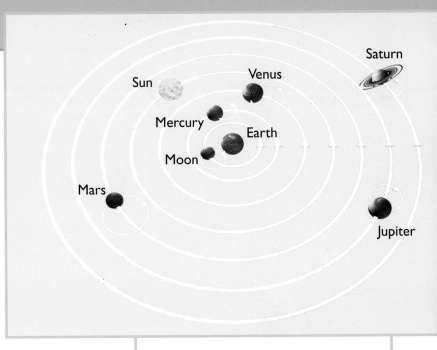

Aristotle imagined the universe this way, with the earth at the center.

Unfortunately for Galileo, the Arno River flooded in the middle of his journey by horse and carriage from Florence to Pisa. His arrival was delayed so much that he failed to deliver his first six lectures, and was fined part of his salary. It was a bad start to his career at the university.

Aristotelian mathematics

Once he had reached the University of Pisa, Galileo was expected to teach the mathematical ideas that were current at the time. These were based on the teachings of Aristotle. They said that the earth was the center of the universe, and that the sun, the moon, and the stars all traveled around the earth, which stayed still. Aristotle also said that while the earth was imperfect and corrupt, or wicked, the heavens were pure and perfect. These ideas were approved by the Church, since the Bible seemed to say the same thing.

THE POWER OF THE CHURCH

During Galileo's lifetime, everyone in Italy was Catholic. The Catholic Church told people how to behave, how to dress, and even how to think. Many of the time's best-known thinkers belonged to Catholic religious orders. Galileo's ideas seemed radical to Church leaders and he came into conflict with the Church later on in his life.

Problems at Pisa

In 1589, teachers at the University of Pisa were expected to wear a toga, the ancient dress of the citizens of Rome, at all times. Galileo thought the toga a nuisance, especially when he was performing experiments. He refused to wear it, working in his normal clothes instead. He ended up being fined even more of his pay.

Yet another conflict arose when Galileo, who was supposed to be teaching Aristotelian mathematics, suggested that Aristotle's ideas about falling objects were incorrect. Aristotle had said that a heavy object would fall faster than a light one. But Galileo had noticed that hailstones of different sizes all hit the ground at the same time during a storm, so Aristotle's theory might not necessarily be true.

TESTING ARISTOTLE

Galileo was not the first to have questioned Aristotle's ideas on falling objects. In 1553, Giovanni Battista Benedetti had published details of a similar experiment, and Flemish engineer Simon Stevin had made the same test in 1586. Whether Galileo knew of these experiments is not certain.

Simon Stevin had tested Aristotle's ideas about the speed at which objects fell, and proved them wrong, three years before Galileo did the same.

Proving a point

In the center of Pisa is a famous tower. Instead of standing up straight, as most towers do, it leans to one side. This makes it perfect for dropping objects of various weights to the ground, to see if they hit the earth below at different times. The story goes that Galileo arranged a public experiment at Pisa's leaning tower, dropping various balls from the top of the tower to demonstrate that he was right and Aristotle was wrong.

When dropped, the heavier ball hit the ground first. The Aristotelian **philosophers** let out a sigh of relief, but Galileo did not accept that he had been wrong: "Aristotle says that a 100-pound ball falling from a height of 100 *braccia* [a *braccio* was one arm's length] hits the ground before a 1-pound ball has fallen 1 *braccio*. I say they arrive at the same time. You find on making the test that the larger ball beats the smaller one by two inches [about 5 centimeters]. Now, behind these two inches you want to hide Aristotle's 99 *braccia* and, speaking only of my tiny error, remain silent about his enormous mistake." Galileo was saying that even though he had been slightly wrong, he was still much closer to the truth than was Aristotle. Galileo had challenged the ideas of Aristotle in public. His outspoken views were starting to make him unpopular with his colleagues.

The Leaning Tower of Pisa is where Galileo is said to have dropped cannonballs in an effort to prove Aristotle wrong.

Life in Padua

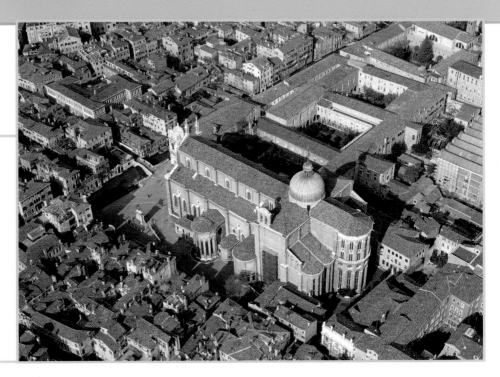

This view shows modern-day Padua. Galileo lived and worked there from 1592 to 1610.

Galileo had made too many enemies at Pisa, and in 1592 he left the university for a new job at the University of Padua, in the the Venetian Republic. He was now earning a respectable salary. The money was welcome, because Galileo's father had died the year before, leaving him as head of the family. Galileo was suddenly responsible for many new expenses: **dowry** payments to his sister Virginia's husband; living costs for his mother and sixteen-year-old brother Michelangelo; and payments to the convent in which his other sister, Livia, was staying until she could be found a husband.

In Padua, Galileo made friends with some of the Venetian Republic's leading figures. As his reputation grew, he was invited to their homes, both as a guest and to take part in public discussions. Once, while staying in the countryside near Padua, Galileo and two of his friends took an afternoon nap in an underground room to keep cool in the heat of the day. This particular room was cooled by air fed through a tunnel that led to a nearby cave. Whether some poisonous gas came into the room from underground, no one knows, but at the end of their nap, all three men felt very ill. One died almost immediately, and the second lasted only a short time. Only Galileo survived, but for the rest of his life, he was plagued by illness.

Galileo and Marina Gamba

While at Padua, Galileo met Marina Gamba, who was to be the mother of his children. Galileo lived in a house on Padua's Borgo dei Vignali (now called Via Galileo Galilei), and Marina lived in Venice. Although they had three children together, Galileo and Marina never married. When Marina became pregnant with Galileo's first child, Virginia, he moved her to a house on Padua's Ponte Corvo, just a few minutes' walk from his own. Virginia was baptized in August 1600; her sister, Livia, was baptized a year later; and Galileo's son, Vincenzio, in August 1606. Galileo was very close to his children, and came to rely on Virginia in particular later on in his life.

Galileo made more profit from sales of the booklet explaining how his geometric compass could be used than he did from the invention itself.

THE GEOMETRIC COMPASS

While Galileo was teaching at Padua, he invented the **geometric compass.** This was a device that functioned as an early pocket calculator, allowing users to make complicated mathematical calculations quickly. Galileo made the first few compasses himself, but paid a craftsman to make the rest. In 1607, he published a booklet explaining how the compass was to be used and dedicated it to his student, Cosimo de' Medici, the future ruler of Florence.

A Marvelous Invention

Galileo had continued to work on his ideas about motion while teaching at Padua. He studied cannonball flights and helped to devise the mathematical calculations for the science of **ballistics,** proving that objects fired from guns follow a predictable route, and travel farthest when fired from an upward angle of 45 degrees.

One of Galileo's students at this time was Cosimo de' Medici, the son of the ruler of Florence. Galileo traveled back to Florence during his vacations to teach Cosimo mathematics. The Grand Duchess Christina, Cosimo's mother, began to take an interest in Galileo's career; when he traveled back to Florence, he often did so in the Grand Duchess's **litter.**

This is an artist's impression of Galileo noting what he could see from his spyglass, which would soon be renamed the telescope.

Improving the spyglass

In 1609, Galileo's investigations took a completely different direction. During the summer of that year, he heard rumors of a new Dutch invention called a **spyglass,** that allowed objects viewed from far away to be seen as though they were near.

Galileo immediately realized the advantage such a device could give to military commanders. He made a spyglass of his own, more powerful than any that had been heard of at the time, and presented it to the rulers of Venice. Even the oldest among them took turns climbing the highest bell towers in the city, where they were amazed to be able to see clearly ships on the horizon that were invisible to the naked eye.

This tower in Padua was home to Galileo's observatory. Much of Galileo's later work was done from the roof of his house in Florence, from which he had a clear view of the heavens.

A job for life

The rulers of Venice were delighted by Galileo's gift. They wanted him to continue making spyglasses for them, and hoped that he would make other new and useful discoveries as well. Galileo's job at Padua University was made his for life. This was good news, because Galileo's responsibilities had increased: his three children had been born, and his sister Livia had found a husband. When Livia married in 1601, Galileo paid for the ceremony and wedding feast, paid the **dowry** to her husband, and bought Livia's dress. Despite these new demands on him, Galileo later said that the time he spent in Padua was the happiest of his life.

THE THERMOSCOPE

While at Padua, Galileo invented the thermoscope, an early thermometer. Galileo's thermoscope was a tube attached to a flask containing liquid. The liquid rose up the tube in higher temperatures. It also reacted with the air pressure at the open end of the tube, so the thermoscope worked as a barometer as well.

17

Telescopic Discoveries

These are two of Galileo's drawings of the face of the moon. They show the craters and ridges on the moon that proved Aristotle was wrong when he said the heavens were perfect.

In Galileo's words:

"It is like the face of the Earth itself," he wrote, *"which is marked here and there with chains of mountains and depths of valleys."*

(Galileo, describing the moon as seen through a telescope, in *The Starry Messenger*)

As the summer of 1609 began to turn to autumn, the days became shorter and shorter. In the early darkness one evening, Galileo happened to focus one of his **spyglasses** on the face of the moon. The strange features that met his eye had never before been seen. Galileo became determined to grind lenses for increasingly more powerful telescopes.

By the end of November 1609, Galileo had managed to make lenses twice as powerful as those in the spyglass that had so amazed the rulers of Venice. The lenses were able to magnify objects to twenty times their normal size. Using his new invention, Galileo spent much of December making detailed drawings of the face of the moon.

Galileo then turned his attention to the stars. During his time there were thought to be two kinds of stars: "fixed stars" that stayed in the same relative positions in the sky, and "wandering stars," or planets—Mercury, Venus, Mars, Jupiter, and Saturn.

He became especially interested in the wandering stars, and spent much of the winter making drawings of what he saw through his telescope. Early in January 1610, Galileo made an extraordinary discovery: around Jupiter were "four planets never [before] seen, from the beginning of the world."

The Starry Messenger

Galileo quickly wrote a book on his discoveries in the heavens, called *The Starry Messenger*, which sold out within a week. He dedicated it to his former student, Cosimo de' Medici, who had become Cosimo II, Grand Duke of Tuscany, in 1609 when his father died. Galileo also named the planets, which are actually the moons of Jupiter, the Medicean stars. He sent Cosimo a copy of *The Starry Messenger*, accompanied by a telescope through which he would be able to see the Medicean stars.

Galileo's flattery of Cosimo II had the desired effect. In the late spring of 1610, Galileo was appointed chief mathematician of the University of Pisa and **philosopher** to the grand duke of Tuscany. After almost eighteen years in Padua, Galileo was about to return home to Florence in triumph.

The British **Ambassador** to Venice, Sir Henry Wotton, wrote to King James I about *The Starry Messenger*, saying that the author would be *"either exceeding famous or exceeding ridiculous."*

Looking through his telescope, Galileo noticed that Saturn was not perfectly round, but instead had what he thought looked like "ears." Galileo was seeing what we now know are Saturn's rings.

Life in Florence

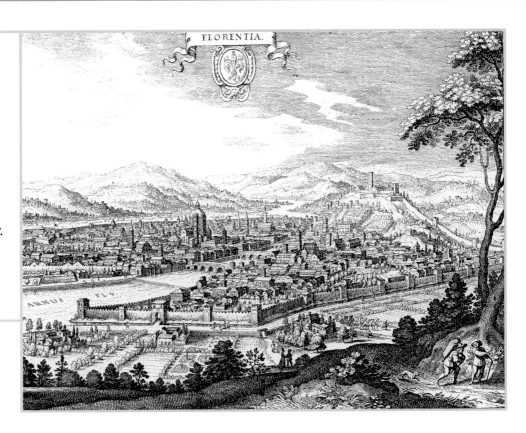

FLORENTIA.

During Galileo's lifetime, Florence was growing rapidly, and was one of the most powerful states in Italy.

When Galileo headed south to Florence in September of 1610 to begin his job as court mathematician and **philosopher,** he took his nine-year-old daughter Livia along on the journey. His older daughter, Virginia, had gone ahead the previous autumn with Galileo's mother. Vincenzio had stayed with his mother, Marina Gamba, in Padua.

As soon as he arrived in Florence, Galileo again set up his telescopes. He found the winter air of Florence made him very unwell, though—since his nap in the underground room in Padua, he had suffered poor health almost every winter. As the winter drew to a close, he complained to a friend that his illness had "during the last three months reduced me to such a state of weakness... that I have been practically confined to my bed." Nonetheless, Galileo continued to make observations of the planets. He also raced to make as many telescopes as possible for sale in the rest of Europe, because astronomers with less powerful telescopes that could not see as much as Galileo's were beginning to question his discoveries.

Galileo visits Rome

As part of the defense of his discoveries, Galileo journeyed to Rome. He traveled in Grand Duke Cosimo's **litter,** and each night set up his telescope to map the "stars" of Jupiter. Galileo arrived in Rome to a warm welcome: he gave talks and visited the homes of many religious leaders, including even Pope Paul V. Galileo also became a member of the prestigious **Lyncean Academy,** a group of the greatest thinkers of the day. The academy had been set up by Federico Cesi, a Roman noble with great interest in mathematics. From this time on, it would be the academy that published Galileo's work.

Pope Paul V met with Galileo when he visited Rome in 1611. The pope was so impressed that he promised to be Galileo's friend and supporter for life.

Most significant of all Galileo's meetings in Rome, though it may not have seemed so at the time, was with a high-ranking Catholic priest, a **cardinal** named Maffeo Barberini. The two met again in Florence that autumn, when Cardinal Barberini was Grand Duke Cosimo's guest, and Galileo took part in an after-dinner debate about the nature of floating objects. Barberini joined in with the debate and was impressed by Galileo. Cardinal Barberini appears again later in the story of Galileo's life; the next time, though, his appearance is rather less friendly.

> *"I pray the Lord God to preserve you, because men of great value like you deserve to live a long time to the benefit of the public."*
>
> (Cardinal Barberini, later to be Pope Urban VIII, in a letter to Galileo. From *Galileo, Courtier,* Mario Biagioli, 1993)

The Church and Science

In seventeenth-century Italy, the Catholic Church controlled almost all aspects of life. Nearly everyone was brought up a Catholic, and believed that unless they accepted the teachings of the Church, it would be impossible for them to get to heaven.

The head of the Church was the pope, who in the Catholic faith is thought to be God's representative on Earth. The pope was therefore able to tell people the true meaning of passages in the Bible, which contained all of God's words to his followers. Any interpretation of the Bible that differed from the pope's went against the Catholic Church, and therefore against God.

The Counter-Reformation

All this had recently been challenged by a German named Martin Luther. He said that a person should be able to make his or her own interpretation of the Bible. In northern Europe, especially some German states, and in the Netherlands and England, this idea—known as **Protestantism**—took hold, and people rejected Catholicism. To fight back, the Church began a movement called the **Counter-Reformation.** This aimed to keep more people from converting to Protestantism, and to win worshipers back to the Catholic faith.

This painting shows Martin Luther, one of the first people to challenge openly the Catholic Church's right to interpret the Bible for Christians.

One of the main ways in which the Church ensured that people remained good Catholics was through the **Inquisition.** In Italy, all towns had a local inquisitor whose job was to make sure that the Church's teachings were followed. If the inquisitor suspected someone of not following the Church's teachings, he was able to question them, using torture if necessary. Anyone who was found guilty was called a **heretic,** and would almost certainly be burned at the stake.

These inquisitors torture a confession out of a suspected heretic.

The Church and the universities

The Church controlled life at Italy's universities just as it controlled life everywhere else. It was especially strict about areas in which the Bible seemed to give guidance on what was true. One example of this was the idea that the earth was motionless at the center of the universe, with all the stars and planets moving around it. Among other passages, the Bible's Psalm 104 seemed especially clear: "O Lord my God... Thou fixed the earth upon its foundation, not to be moved forever." During Galileo's lifetime—in 1600, the year his older daughter, Virginia, was born—a Dominican friar named Giordano Bruno had been burned at the stake in Rome for claiming that the earth moved around the sun. Now Galileo himself was being led toward exactly the same dangerous view by the amazing things he discovered with his telescope.

Under Suspicion

This is the book De Revolutionibus, *by Nicolaus Copernicus. Copernicus thought the sun, rather than the earth, might be the center of the universe.*

The idea that the earth went around the sun had first been put forward by the Polish astronomer Nicolaus Copernicus in 1543. Copernicus's book *De Revolutionibus* suggested that the earth turned on its **axis** once a day, and traveled around the sun once a year. Galileo would have been aware of these ideas, and everything that he had discovered using his telescopes seemed to him to suggest that they were true.

Galileo knew that the Church supported Aristotle's idea that the earth remained motionless at the heart of the universe. He had probably heard reports from Rome about Giordano Bruno being burned at the stake for disagreeing. Galileo was also a good Catholic, who wanted to agree with the Church. But he could not deny the evidence of his own eyes and his new scientific method.

The letter to Castelli

In 1613, Galileo wrote to his student Benedetto Castelli about the problems caused by the conflict between Copernican ideas and the Bible. It was common for letters such as this to be copied between friends so that they could share ideas, and Galileo's letter was copied several times.

Galileo's evidence

- Neither the moon nor the sun was perfect, as Aristotle claimed. The moon had mountains and valleys, and the sun had sunspots.

- Jupiter's moons proved that not everything was in orbit around the earth as the Bible seemed to suggest, since they orbited Jupiter.

- The phases of Venus, or the different ways Venus looked at different times of the year, showed that it was in orbit around the sun, not the earth.

An inaccurate copy fell into the hands of the **Inquisition** in Rome, probably sent there by Galileo's enemies. He was forced to send an accurate copy to the Inquisition to clear his name, but still he found himself suspected of going against the Church's teachings. Galileo decided to travel to Rome to defend himself.

However, at least one of Galileo's worries was cleared up around this time. Respectable Italian families often sent their daughters to a convent until they were found a husband, and Galileo had been trying to get his daughters into the convent of San Matteo near Florence for some time. In October of 1613, thirteen-year-old Virginia and her twelve-year-old sister, Livia, were finally admitted to live there.

Nicolaus Copernicus was a Polish priest who observed the heavens with the naked eye before the telescope was invented. He based De Revolutionibus *on these observations.*

By the time Galileo left his daughters to visit Rome in 1615–16, he had expanded his letter to Castelli into what became known as the *Letter to the Grand Duchess Christina*, the mother of his former student, Cosimo de' Medici. He had also written long letters defending his ideas to influential figures in the Church. Others had begun to agree with Copernicus, too, including Father Paolo Foscarini, who published a pamphlet saying that it was possible to support Copernican ideas with passages of the Bible.

A Warning

The ideas of Copernicus now had supporters in the universities and the churches. But the discussion about the conflict between Copernican theory and the Bible was slowly turning into a battle between science and the Church, at least in Galileo's mind. He agreed with a remark he had once heard from **Cardinal** Cesare Baronio, a senior Catholic, who said that the Bible was a book about how people go to heaven; not about how heaven goes. Galileo's letter to Benedetto

When the edict of 1616 was issued, Galileo's views suddenly became dangerous.

Castelli in 1613 shows how frustrating he must have found the use of tiny passages in the Bible to contradict whole new areas of knowledge, "above all in astronomy, of which so little notice is taken [in the Bible] that the names of none of the planets are mentioned. Surely if the intention of the [Bible was] to teach the people astronomy, [it] would not have passed over the subject so completely."

The Edict of 1616

In February of 1616, a council of Catholic experts issued an **edict,** or order, telling the **Inquisition** that the idea of the sun being at the center of the universe was **heretical.** Anyone now holding a Copernican view of the universe would be tried before the Inquisition. They could be questioned, tortured, imprisoned, and put to death if found guilty.

Soon afterward, Copernicus's book *De Revolutionibus* was banned until it could be altered; Father Foscarini's pamphlet defending Copernican beliefs was banned for being heretical; and Galileo himself was called to account for his views.

Galileo escaped being accused of **heresy** by the Inquisition. Instead, on the orders of the pope, he was summoned to the house of Cardinal Bellarmine, an important leader in the Church. The cardinal told Galileo that he must not "hold or defend" Copernican theory, or he would be called before the Inquisition and charged with heresy. To argue with this decision would probably have cost Galileo his life. He had to agree.

Galileo returned home to Florence in plenty of time to see his beloved daughter, Virginia, take her vows as a nun on October 4, 1616. She would now never marry, and instead would spend her whole life in the convent. To mark this new beginning, she took a new name, Sister Maria Celeste.

This woman hesitates before entering a convent. As a nun, Sister Maria Celeste would have had a hard life, with little to eat and almost no comforts, but plenty of work and praying.

The Comet Debate

Galileo returned home from Rome in 1616 and got back to work on his ideas about motion, which he had all but abandoned in 1609. Then, in September of 1618, Galileo was ill again, and stopped working. Almost immediately, his attention was drawn back to the heavens. From September to November, three comets were seen in the skies above Florence. Galileo was not well enough to leave bed and examine the comets through his telescope, but he began a written argument on the nature of comets with a **Jesuit** priest and mathematician, Father Horatio Grassi.

An artist's impression of a comet in the seventeenth century shows it as a "shooting star." In fact, comets are made of ice and dust surrounded by gas. In 1618, three comets were seen above Florence, but Galileo was too ill to view them through his telescope.

The argument over comets dragged on for several years. By now, both of Galileo's daughters were nuns in the convent of San Matteo. When Marina Gamba died in 1619, twelve-year-old Vincenzio was left without a legal **guardian.** Since Marina and Galileo had never married, Vincenzio could not be known as Galileo's son until he was finally recognized as **legitimate** by Grand Duke Cosimo II in June 1619.

In 1620, Galileo's mother died at the age of 82. Then, in January 1621, Pope Paul V died of a stroke. A new pope, Gregory XV, was chosen, but he was in frail health and seemed unlikely to live for much longer. Finally, in February of 1621, Grand Duke Cosimo died, succeeded by his ten-year-old son, Ferdinando II. Ferdinando not only inherited his father's title and lands, he also inherited his court mathematician and **philosopher:** Galileo.

This is the cover of The Assayer. *Most books at that time were written in Latin, a language intellectuals could understand, but Galileo wrote in Italian so that ordinary people could read his work.*

The Assayer

Slowed down by illness himself, Galileo continued to work on *The Assayer,* his book about the comet debate. By October of 1622, he had delivered the final manuscript to the **Lyncean Academy** in Rome for publication. But when the printing was almost finished the following summer, it was halted by dramatic events. Gregory XV had died, and a new pope was elected. In what seemed a stroke of great good luck, the new pope was an old ally of Galileo's, the former **Cardinal** Maffeo Barberini. He took the name Pope Urban VIII. Galileo immediately dedicated *The Assayer* to Pope Urban, hoping to win his ideas favor in Rome.

Galileo Visits the Pope

Today, Vatican City, in the heart of Rome, is still the headquarters of the Catholic Church.

Galileo and the new pope had been exchanging letters for years. Galileo had kept him informed of new ideas and sent copies of each new book. Barberini, in turn, had recently written thanking Galileo for helping his nephew Francesco through his studies at Pisa University.

As pope, Urban remained interested in Galileo's ideas, and after *The Assayer* was published, it was read aloud to him at each mealtime. He was fascinated, and invited Galileo to visit Rome. Once again, illness had confined Galileo to bed, and it was spring of 1624 before he was able to travel. The day after he arrived, Galileo met Urban, and over the course of the next five weeks the two met five more times. They walked together in the Vatican gardens, talking for hours. Among the things Urban and Galileo must have discussed was the **edict** of 1616, forbidding the Copernican view of the universe.

As far as Urban was concerned, the idea that the earth orbited the sun was simply an idea. Considered in this way, it could not harm the Catholic faith, and could be discussed by Catholic scholars such as Galileo. Only if the Copernican version of the universe was taught as absolute truth would the Church be forced to act.

This engraving shows Pope Urban VIII. He was pope from 1623 to 1644.

Galileo left Rome to return home on June 8, 1624. He took with him a personal letter from Urban VIII to Grand Duke Ferdinando II, praising Galileo as a "great man whose fame shines in the heavens and goes on Earth far and wide." He also took with him the idea that it might be possible to reopen the debate about how the universe worked.

The *Letter to Ingoli*

Before writing a full-length book on how he believed the universe worked, Galileo tested the water with a short reply to an article that had appeared in 1616 challenging his views. In the *Letter to Ingoli,* he argued for the Copernican view, but made it clear that he was not claiming it to be true: "I do not undertake this task with the aim of supporting as true a proposition that has already been declared suspect and repugnant," he said in the introduction. Instead, he said he was showing the world that Catholic thinkers understood all the arguments, not just those the Church recognized.

Dialogo

The cover of Galileo's book Dialogue *is complete with a dedication to Grand Duke Ferdinando II.*

Galileo's *Letter to Ingoli* reached Rome in December of 1624. By the end of the month, the pope had heard at least part of it, and had not responded to its contents in anger. Galileo decided this must mean that the way was now clear for him to write a full-length book about the different ideas of how the universe was organized. It was a book that he had been planning for years. It was to take the form of an imaginary four-day discussion among three friends, who have met in Venice to consider scientific ideas. Salviati is a scientist like Galileo himself; Sagredo is a gentleman who is open to being persuaded; and Simplicio is a pompous Aristotelian **philosopher.** The book was called *Dialogo,* or *Dialogue Concerning the Two Chief World Systems.*

Galileo continued working on *Dialogue* for the next six years. In the meantime, he was interrupted once again by sickness, and by the arrival of his sister-in-law and her eight children in 1627. They might have come to escape the battles of the Thirty Years' War that was raging across Germany, where they lived. Galileo, who was 63 at the time, suddenly had a house full of noisy children, as well as nine extra mouths to feed.

This painting depicts Venice during the plague. The Black Death, or bubonic plague, appeared throughout Europe, North Africa, and the Middle East at various times, and killed one-third of the population.

Dialogue was finally finished late in 1629, but before it could be published, it had to be approved by the Church. Because of its delicate subject matter, Galileo decided to take the book to Rome himself and steer it through the approval process. After visiting Rome in the spring of 1630, Galileo was asked to make changes to small sections. Then, that summer and for the next year, a terrible disease called the **Black Death** raged throughout Europe. Galileo's own brother, Michelangelo, died from the disease in Germany in 1631. Because of the plague, travel was dangerous at the time, so the whole manuscript for the book was never seen again by the same person. Instead, it went to the printer with some parts approved by officials in Rome and other parts approved by officials in Florence. That year, Galileo moved to a house a short distance from his daughters' convent in Arcetri.

Getting published

Dialogue was finally published in February 1632. It was an immediate success, selling out as soon as it left the printer. But trouble was brewing in Rome. Galileo was now 68 years old, and he was about to begin a fight for his life.

33

Trouble at the Vatican

By the time *Dialogue* was published, Urban's rule as pope was in trouble. As well as being a spiritual leader, he was also a political one, and he had used his political power to gain wealth and influence for his family. As a result, Urban had made many enemies among the important families of Italy.

Worse still, Urban was being accused of failing to defend the Catholic faith. A dispute between France and Spain about the right to the Catholic throne of the Holy Roman Empire had been going on for years. Instead of trying to settle the argument between two Catholic countries, Urban had supported the French claim. By the summer of 1632, Urban was so worried about Spanish spies and **assassins** that he had left the Vatican and moved to a summer house outside Rome.

Cardinal Francesco Barberini was appointed a cardinal after his uncle became pope. This was a good example of how Urban used his power to benefit his own family.

CARDINAL FRANCESCO BARBERINI

One of Galileo's most important allies was **Cardinal** Francesco Barberini, the pope's nephew. Francesco had admired Galileo for years, having first gotten to know him while studying under Benedetto Castelli at Pisa. Galileo had taught Castelli. Francesco worked behind the scenes to influence his uncle in Galileo's favor.

There is no evidence that Urban ever read *Dialogue,* but others read it for him. They judged it to be a thinly disguised defense of Copernicus, going against both the **edict** of 1616 and Urban's advice that any discussion dealing with Copernican ideas should be theoretical only. Some thought that the pompous character of Simplicio represented Urban. A paper was also produced that related to the warning Galileo had been given by Cardinal Bellarmine in 1616. This suggested that Galileo had agreed never to discuss Copernican ideas in any way, rather than that he should not "hold or defend" them. Urban felt betrayed: Galileo had never mentioned this warning to him before—probably because it was never actually given to Galileo.

This is an artist's impression of Galileo appearing before Urban VIII in 1633. In fact, Urban remained a figure in the background during Galileo's trial, and the two did not meet while it was going on.

Trouble for Galileo

Galileo found that the pope had suddenly become his enemy. Urban was eager to show that, in this area at least, he was a defender of the Church's teachings. In 1632, Galileo was summoned to appear before the **Inquisition** in Rome, leaving his beloved daughter, Sister Maria Celeste, in charge of his home at Arcetri. Galileo arrived in February 1633, then stayed in the Tuscan **Embassy** for two months before he began to give evidence in April.

"When his Holiness gets something into his head, that is the end of the matter, especially if one is opposing, threatening, or defying him, since then he hardens and shows no respect to anyone. This [the investigation] is really going to be a troublesome affair."
(**Ambassador** Niccolini of the Tuscan Embassy)

Galileo on Trial

Galileo appeared before the Inquisition in Rome. He always thought of himself as a good Catholic, and was horrified to find himself on trial for heresy because of his scientific beliefs.

On Tuesday, April 12, 1633, Galileo stood in the Holy Office of the **Inquisition** in Rome. Before him were two officials and a secretary, whose job was to ask prearranged questions and then report the answers to the Inquisition judges. Galileo would finally be judged by a panel of ten **cardinals,** including Cardinal Francesco Barberini.

The verdict

After hearing Galileo's answers—in which he denied ever having intended to say that Copernicus's ideas were true—the cardinals were unsure what to do. They decided to ask the advice of experts. Unfortunately for Galileo, when the experts reported back, their views were damning. They said that *Dialogue* did defend Copernican theory: Galileo was guilty as charged.

Still, the cardinals felt it would be better if Galileo could be dealt with without a formal trial. The Church had, after all, approved *Dialogue* before publication, and would look stupid if it tried to punish an author for writing a book it had allowed to be published. The pope agreed.

This seventeenth-century painting shows Galileo abjuring his Copernican beliefs. Pope Urban VIII had the text of Galileo's abjuration read out publicly all over the Catholic world to humiliate Galileo.

On May 10, Galileo appeared again before the Inquisition, having spent three weeks imprisoned at the Vatican. He was there to **abjure,** or renounce, the Copernican view of the world. He gave the Inquisition a written document in which he said that he now realized *Dialogue* accidentally suggested that the Copernican view was correct, even though the Church rightly said that it was incorrect. After his abjuration, Galileo was allowed to return to the Tuscan **Embassy.**

The sentence

Arguments went on within the Church for weeks, and it was June 22, 1633, before Galileo's sentence was announced. The Inquisition found Galileo guilty of "heinous [terrible] crimes." He was "vehemently suspect of **heresy.**" *Dialogue* was banned, and Galileo was to be imprisoned for life. On his knees, dressed in the white robes of a regretful sinner, Galileo abjured anti-Catholic beliefs, and was taken down to be locked in his cell.

> *"It is a fearful thing to have to do with the Inquisition. The poor man has come back more dead than alive."*
>
> (**Ambassador** Niccolini of the Tuscan Embassy, on Galileo's condition after his abjuration.)

The Prisoner

Within days of Galileo's imprisonment, his sentence was softened. **Cardinal** Francesco Barberini, who had not supported the guilty verdict, persuaded his uncle to allow Galileo to return to the Tuscan **Embassy.** From there, **Ambassador** Niccolini fought for Galileo to be allowed to go home. Urban would not agree, but he allowed Galileo to serve the next five months of his sentence at the home of the archbishop of Siena. Although still technically a prisoner of the **Inquisition,** as he would remain until the day he died, Galileo was more than halfway home.

Meanwhile, the **black market** price of *Dialogue* rose and rose. It remained banned by the Catholic Church until 1822, 65 years after other books supporting Copernicus had been taken off the Church's **Index of Banned Books.**

Recovering from the ordeal

When he reached the home of the archbishop of Siena, 69-year-old Galileo was exhausted. The archbishop, who was also a mathematician, tried to interest Galileo in scientific problems, including the difficulty he was having in recasting the ancient bell of his cathedral. Galileo was also helped to recover by the regular letters he received from his daughter, Sister Maria Celeste. She wrote often, telling him all the details from home.

Galileo became involved in trying to solve the problem of how the bell of this cathedral in Siena could be recast.

In Galileo's words:

Galileo said at the end of his life that *Two New Sciences* was *"superior to everything else of mine,"* because it contained *"results which I consider the most important of all my studies."*

This page is from Galileo's last book, Two New Sciences.

A new book

While staying in Siena, Galileo began work on his last great book, *Two New Sciences*. In it, Galileo returned to the ideas that had interested him on and off for over twenty years: the sciences of mechanics and motion. *Two New Sciences* was again an imaginary discussion, among the same three friends—Salviati, Sagredo, and Simplicio—as in the banned *Dialogue*. The discussion takes place in the Venetian **Arsenale.** Over the course of a four-day debate, they examine the behavior of moving objects.

COLLECTING EVIDENCE

Two New Sciences was based on weeks of experiments Galileo performed in Siena. He built complicated devices that allowed him to measure carefully the speed at which balls of various weights moved along slopes. To measure tiny lengths of time, he used water: the amount of water that dripped steadily into a cup represented a certain amount of time passing. Galileo's careful observation and experimentation helped to establish the modern practices used by scientists today, in which theories are thoroughly tested to see if they are true.

Galileo's Last Days

Galileo's supporters continued to campaign for his return home, and in December of 1633, he was finally allowed to return to his house in Arcetri. Nearby was the convent of San Matteo, in which his beloved daughters lived. Galileo was still not allowed visitors and was forbidden ever to teach, but at last he was back home.

The sadness was not over, though. Sister Maria Celeste had been ill on and off for the whole of Galileo's absence in Rome. In March 1634, she fell ill with **dysentery,** and some time during the second night of April, she died. Galileo was beside himself with grief.

Galileo found himself alone, with nothing to do but work on *Two New Sciences.* When the book was finished, his friends found it almost impossible to find a publisher.

This was Galileo's home in Arcetri, where he died in 1642.

Justus Sustermans painted Galileo as an old man in about 1636. In the year Galileo died, another great scientist, the Englishman Isaac Newton, was born. Newton would base his revolutionary work on some of Galileo's ideas.

Galileo's work was too risky for any Italian publisher to print. Finally, the book was smuggled over the Alps to the Netherlands, a **Protestant** country where the Catholic Church had no influence. It was published in spring of 1638, but by the time a copy reached Galileo he could not read it. After years of peering into telescopes, he was almost blind.

The death of Galileo

For companionship, Grand Duke Ferdinando sent Galileo a young man named Vincenzio Viviani, who was a gifted mathematician. In 1641, they were joined by Evangelista Torricelli, who later invented the barometer. That year, Galileo designed a **pendulum** device that could keep time. It was a forerunner to the pendulum clock.

By November, Galileo was in bed with a fever similar to those he had suffered every winter for years. This time it was fatal. On January 8, 1642, just short of his 78th birthday, one of the world's greatest scientists was dead.

THE SECRET SKELETON

When Galileo died, Pope Urban forbade a ceremonial burial. Galileo's friend Viviani campaigned for a fitting monument, but never succeeded. When Viviani himself died, he was buried next to Galileo. Galileo was finally allowed a monument 95 years after his death. When his grave was opened, though, onlookers were amazed to discover three skeletons. Viviani had secretly moved the body of Sister Maria Celeste there. Ashamed at not providing Galileo with the monument he deserved, Viviani had done the next best thing. He had made sure the great scientist rested forever next to his daughter.

Galileo's Legacy

An early pendulum clock was designed by Galileo. This engraving was based on a sketch by Galileo's son, Vincenzio, who built the clock after Galileo's death.

Most of Galileo's discoveries happened when he was a very young man, but his fame outlived him. Galileo was not only a great astronomer and scientist, he was also a brilliant mathematician and a talented, successful inventor. The list of Galileo's achievements is impressive and adds up to an amazing legacy:

• He was one of the first people to realize that the speed at which objects fall is not related to their weight, but to other forces. This idea is central to our understanding of how **gravity** works.

• Galileo built the first telescopes capable of observing the sky at night, and using them, provided the earliest evidence that the earth was not at the center of the universe. Galileo discovered the moons of Jupiter and many other features of our solar system.

• He made valuable discoveries in the science of **ballistics,** developing calculations that are still used today.

• He was the creator of numerous inventions: the **hydrostatic balance;** the **geometric compass;** the thermoscope; and the first clock ever to use the motion of a **pendulum** to keep time.

The search for proof

Galileo was the first scientist to insist—at all times—that there had to be evidence for an idea before it could be considered true. Many times in his life, Galileo complained about **philosophers** who simply followed what they had been taught, and therefore gave confident, but incorrect, answers to questions. Galileo said that these men would have been better off giving the only true answer they could have given, which was: "I do not know." Galileo preferred to test his ideas using experiments, explaining his results mathematically. His methods opened the doors to science as we know it, and it is this way of approaching new ideas that is his greatest legacy.

This monument to Galileo was set up in 1737 in the church of Santa Croce in Florence.

"Because Galileo saw this [that ideas need to be tested], and particularly because he drummed it into the scientific world, he is the father of modern physics—indeed of modern science altogether."

(Albert Einstein, one of the greatest scientists of the twentieth century)

Timeline

1543	Nicolaus Copernicus publishes *De Revolutionibus* in Poland.
1564	Galileo Galilei is born in Pisa, Tuscany. William Shakespeare is born in England.
1581	Galileo goes to study at the University of Pisa.
1585	Galileo leaves the University of Pisa without a degree and returns to his father's house in Florence.
1589	Galileo gets a teaching job at Pisa. He begins his studies on motion and begins to make enemies among the Aristotelian **philosophers.**
1591	Galileo's father, Vincenzio, dies.
1592	Galileo takes a job teaching at the University of Padua in the Venetian Republic.
1600	Giordano Bruno is burned at the stake for claiming that the earth orbits the sun. Virginia Galilei, daughter of Galileo and Marina Gamba, is born.
1601	Galileo and Marina Gamba have another daughter, Livia Galilei.
1606	Galileo and Marina Gamba's son, Vincenzio Galilei, is born.
1609	Galileo begins making increasingly powerful telescopes, and starts to observe the heavens.
1610	Galileo discovers the moons of Jupiter; *The Starry Messenger* is published. Galileo is appointed chief mathematician and philosopher to the grand duke of Tuscany.
1611	Galileo visits Rome.
1616	**Edict** from Rome forbids Copernican theory. Virginia Galilei becomes nun and takes the name Sister Maria Celeste.
1617	Livia Galilei becomes nun; known as Sister Archangela.
1618–23	Debate rages about the nature of comets.
1619	Marina Gamba, mother of Galileo's children, dies.
1623	Maffeo Barberini becomes Pope Urban VIII. *The Assayer* is published.
1624	Galileo visits Urban in Rome.
1631	Michelangelo, Galileo's brother, dies of the plague in Germany.
1632	*Dialogue* is published.
1633	Galileo on trial for **heresy.** *Dialogue* is banned.
1634	Sister Maria Celeste dies at the age of 33.

1638	Galileo's *Two New Sciences* is published in the Netherlands.
1639	Vincenzio Viviani arrives to keep Galileo company.
1641	Evangelista Torricelli joins Galileo at Arcetri.
1642	Galileo dies at the age of 77.
	Isaac Newton is born in England.
1643	Galileo's son builds an early **pendulum** clock, according to his father's design.
1644	Pope Urban VIII dies.
1822	*Dialogue* is taken off the **Index of Banned Books.**

More Books to Read

Hightower, Paul W. *Galileo: Astronomer and Physicist.* Berekley Heights, N.J.: Enslow Publishers, 1997.

MacLachlan, James. *Galileo Galilei: First Physicist.* New York: Oxford University Press, 1997.

White, Michael. *Galileo Galilei: Inventor, Astronomer, and Rebel.* Woodbridge, Conn.: Blackbirch Press, 1999.

Glossary

abjure to take back or solemnly deny an opinion

ambassador person who represents one country's government to that of another

Arsenale shipyard in which the great fleets of the Venetian navy were built

assassin hired killer

axis imaginary line through the center of the earth around which the earth rotates

ballistics study of firing objects, as from guns or cannons

Black Death deadly disease carried between humans by fleas; also called the plague

black market illegal trade in goods, often in goods that have been banned

cardinal high-ranking official in the Catholic Church

Counter-Reformation movement within the Catholic Church that aimed to make sure people followed the Church's teachings

counterweight part of a weighing device that balances the item being weighed

dowry payment made by a bride's family to her new husband

dysentery disease of the intestines causing stomach pain and severe diarrhea

edict formal decision or command

embassy office of an ambassador and his or her staff

geometric compass device that used two rules marked with measurements to make complicated mathematical calculations

geometry branch of mathematics concerned with shapes

gravity natural force that attracts objects to one another

guardian person who has responsibility for another

harmony combination of several musical notes played at the same time

heresy going against the teachings of the Catholic Church

heretic person who goes against the teachings of the Catholic Church

hydrostatic balance device for weighing things using water as the counterweight

Index of Banned Books list of books that were considered dangerous and therefore were forbidden by the Catholic Church

Inquisition group formed during the Counter-Reformation that made sure people followed the teachings of the Catholic Church by punishing heretics

Jesuit religious order that is part of the Catholic Church

legitimate recognized within the law

litter device for carrying a person or people

logic method of reasoning or arguing in which one idea develops from another

Lyncean Academy group of leading thinkers on a variety of subjects that existed in Italy during the seventeenth century

mechanics branch of science that deals with movement and how machines work

monastery place where monks live together as a community

pendulum weight that hangs down from a fixed point and can swing freely from side to side

philosopher person who studies the history of ideas and creates new ideas about truth and knowledge

philosophy use of reason and argument to seek truth and knowledge

Protestantism religious movement based on the idea that people should be free to interpret the Bible for themselves

spyglass early telescope

tension degree of force to stretch two connected objects apart

Index